Rockwell Media Center
Whittlesey Drive
Bethel, CT 06801

Benjamin Franklin

Steve Goldsworthy

LET'S READ
AV²
BY WEIGL™
ADDED VALUE • AUDIO VISUAL

www.av2books.com

LET'S READ
AV²
BY WEIGL™
ADDED VALUE • AUDIO VISUAL

Go to **www.av2books.com**, and enter this book's unique code.

BOOK CODE

J459011

AV² by Weigl brings you media enhanced books that support active learning.

AV² provides enriched content that supplements and complements this book. Weigl's AV² books strive to create inspired learning and engage young minds in a total learning experience.

Your AV² Media Enhanced books come alive with...

Audio
Listen to sections of the book read aloud.

Video
Watch informative video clips.

Embedded Weblinks
Gain additional information for research.

Try This!
Complete activities and hands-on experiments.

Key Words
Study vocabulary, and complete a matching word activity.

Quizzes
Test your knowledge.

Slide Show
View images and captions, and prepare a presentation.

... and much, much more!

Published by AV² by Weigl
350 5th Avenue, 59th Floor New York, NY 10118
Websites: www.av2books.com www.weigl.com

Library of Congress Control Number: 2014934866

ISBN 978-1-4896-1050-8 (hardcover)
ISBN 978-1-4896-1051-5 (softcover)
ISBN 978-1-4896-1052-2 (single user eBook)
ISBN 978-1-4896-1053-9 (multi-user eBook)

Printed in the United States of America in North Mankato, Minnesota
1 2 3 4 5 6 7 8 9 0 18 17 16 15 14

052014
WEP150314

Project Coordinator: Jared Siemens
Designer: Ana María Vidal

CONTENTS

Who Is Benjamin Franklin?

Benjamin Franklin was one of the Founding Fathers of the United States. He is known as a great man. He helped the United States become a country. Franklin studied how things worked. He came up with ideas that had never been thought of before. This helped him to create many useful things.

What Is a Founding Father?

As a Founding Father Benjamin Franklin fought to free the American colonies from the rule of Great Britain. This freedom led the colonies to form the United States of America. Franklin helped create the laws for this new country. These laws are called the U.S. Constitution.

Growing Up

Benjamin Franklin was born in Boston, Massachusetts, on January 17, 1706. He left school at 10 years of age. He started working as a printer when he was 12 years old.

Learning From Others

Benjamin Franklin learned how to write from reading books. He learned how to be a printer from his older brother James. Franklin started his own newspaper when he was just 16 years old. Franklin started the first American library when he was 25 years old.

Practice Makes Perfect

Benjamin Franklin had many different jobs. He came up with new ideas his whole life. Franklin came up with the idea for the lightning rod when the weather was stormy. The lightning rod keeps tall buildings safe from lightning.

Key Events

Benjamin Franklin served his country as a politician for many years. He saw a war coming between Great Britain and the American colonies. The colonies wanted to make their own choices. They did not want to pay high taxes to Great Britain. Franklin asked the king of Great Britain to let the colonies rule themselves. He was turned down.

Challenges

War broke out between Great Britain and the American colonies in 1775. The British wanted to keep control of the colonies. The colonies needed help to win the war. Franklin asked France to help. France joined the fight against Great Britain. This helped the Americans win the war.

A Nation Is Born

On July 4, 1776, Benjamin Franklin signed the Declaration of Independence with Congress. This declaration said that the American colonies were free from British rule. It also joined the colonies into a new country called the United States of America. Americans celebrate Independence Day on July 4 every year. They do this to remember the day the United States became a country.

Benjamin Franklin Today

Benjamin Franklin is one of the best-known people in American history. His face is found on the $100 bill. Philadelphia, Pennsylvania, is home to the Benjamin Franklin National Memorial. The memorial has a statue of Franklin that is as tall as a two-story building.

BENJAMIN FRANKLIN FACTS

These pages provide detailed information that expands on the interesting facts found in the book. These pages are intended to be used by adults to help young readers round out their knowledge of each historical figure featured in the *Founding Fathers* series.

Pages 4–5

Who Is Benjamin Franklin? Benjamin Franklin was one of America's most influential early citizens. He is sometimes called "the First American" for his contributions to America's creation. His ability to express powerful and universal ideas helped unify the colonies in their fight for liberty. His diplomatic skills were legendary, and his innovative thinking brought many useful advances to American culture. Franklin remains one of the nation's most highly respected figures.

Pages 6–7

What Is a Founding Father? The Founding Fathers of the United States of America played a significant role in forming the country. Though there are no specific requirements for inclusion in this elite group, a Founding Father is typically a person who was involved in, or contributed to, one of the founding events of the United States. These events include the American Revolution, the creation and signing of the Declaration of Independence, and the Constitutional Convention, in which the Constitution of the United States of America was written.

Pages 8–9

Growing Up When Franklin was 15 years old, his brother James started Boston's third newspaper, *The New England Courant*. Ben secretly used the pseudonym Silence Dogood because James refused to publish anything Franklin wrote. When James found out, he punished Franklin. In 1723, Franklin fled Boston and later became an esteemed publisher in Philadelphia.

Pages 10–11

Learning From Others Franklin was greatly influenced by the extensive reading he did throughout his life. His father had originally expected him to study for the clergy. However, he also exposed Franklin to other professions, hoping to end his son's interest in going to sea. Franklin's love of books led him to apprentice for his brother James, who taught him the printing trade.

KEY WORDS

Research has shown that as much as 65 percent of all written material published in English is made up of 300 words. These 300 words cannot be taught using pictures or learned by sounding them out. They must be recognized by sight. This book contains 84 common sight words to help young readers improve their reading fluency and comprehension. This book also teaches young readers several important content words, such as nouns. These words are paired with pictures to aid in learning and improve understanding.

Page	Sight Words First Appearance
4	a, as, been, before, came, country, great, had, he, him, how, ideas, is, man, many, never, of, one, that, the, things, this, thought, to, up, was, with
7	American, are, for, from, new, these, what
9	at, in, left, old, on, school, started, when, years
10	be, books, first, his, just, others, own, write
13	different, keeps, life, makes
14	and, asked, between, did, down, high, let, not, saw, their, they, turned, want
16	help, its, out
19	also, day, do, every, into, it, people, said, were
20	face, found, has, home

Page	Content Words First Appearance
4	Founding Fathers, United States
7	colonies, Constitution, freedom, Great Britain, laws
9	age, Boston, January, Massachusetts, printer
10	brother, library, newspaper
13	buildings, jobs, lightning, practice, rod, weather
14	choices, key events, king, politician, taxes, themselves, war
16	British, challenges, France
19	Congress, declaration, Declaration of Independence, Independence Day, July, nation
20	bill, Benjamin Franklin National Memorial, building, history, memorial, Pennsylvania, Philadelphia, statue

Rockwell Media Center
Whittlesey Drive
Bethel, CT 06801